THE ANTONS ARE HERE

The Pets

Alfa to Zip-zap

BOOK 2

TONY MY-THEN

Personal Development Series

To order other books from the series go to:

www.theantonsarehere.com

Antons®

ISBN: 1902981227

Book 2 in the Personal development series

This book moves on to using capital letters and more complex vowel sounds and' words which, change the sounds of individual letters when those individual letters are used in combination e.g. ch, sh, th.

Before reading on, the student should first be familiar with the Antons' pets and the sounds, noises and calls they make.

Ark ar

One of the Antons' pets

Ark

Ar

ar

Chop ch

One of the Antons' pets

Chop

Ch

ch

Claw ow

One of the Antons' pets

Claw

Aw

aw

Nook 00

One of the Antons' pets

Nook

Oo

oo

Oil

oi

One of the Antons' pets

Oil

Oi

oi

Out ou

One of the Antons' pets

Out

Ou

ou

Owl ow

One of the Antons' pets

Owl

Ow

ow

This'n'that   th

One of the Antons' pets

This'n'that

Th

th

Wish sh

One of the Antons' pets

Wish

Sh

sh

This part of the book moves on to using words which change the sounds of individual letters when those individual letters are used in combination e.g. ch, sh, th.

Before reading on, the student should first be familiar with the Antons' pets and the sounds, noises and calls they make.

Alfa a

1 in a party of 26 Antons

Is it
Alfa?
Yes,
and he
is the
leader.

Bobbin b

2 in a party of 26 Antons

It is
Bobbin
and he
is a
winner.

Clip-clop c

3 in a party of 26 Antons

Is Clip-clop
big?
Yes, and
very
cuddly.

Delta d

4 in a party of 26 Antons

Delta is
not big,
but
she is
very nice.

Epic e

5 in a party of 26 Antons

Can Epic
run?
Yes, and
she can
swim.

Foxtrot F

6 in a party of 26 Antons

Is Foxtrot
six?
Foxtrot is
number
six.

Golf

g

7 in a party of 26 Antons

Yes, Golf
is in
and
he is
going
out.

Hip-hop

h

 in a party of 26 Antons

Hip-hop
is fun,
and he
likes
fish
and chips.

In-off i

In-off
can
run to
the
shop.

Jig-jag j

10 in a party of 26 Antons

Is Jig-jag
ten?
Jig-jag
is number
ten.

Kit-kin k

11 in a party of 26 Antons

Is Kit-kin
fun?
Yes,
and he
likes to
play out.

Lapland I

12 in a party of 26 Antons

Lapland
can sit
on a
big
chair.

Moffin m

13 in a party of 26 Antons

Is Moffin
big?
Yes, and
he likes
his
food.

Nuggin n

14 in a party of 26 Antons

Can
Nuggin jog?
Yes,
all the
way to
the shop.

On-off o

15 in a party of 26 Antons

On-off
can swim
as well
as
a fish.

Papa p

16 in a party of 26 Antons

Papa
can jog
and run,
and he
can be
good fun.

Quin

q

17 in a party of 26 Antons

Quin can
run and
swim.
Can you
run
or swim?

Red r

 in a party of 26 Antons

Red went
and had
fun.
You can
have good
fun too.

Spot

s

19 in a party of 26 Antons

Yes,
Spot-on
went fast.
Can you
go fast
too?

Tip-tap t

 in a party of 26 Antons

Tip-tap
and Red
had fun,
then
went for
a run.

Upton

u

21 in a party of 26 Antons

Upton can
swim fast
with his
goggles on.

Vanilla V

22 in a party of 26 Antons

Is it
Vanilla?
Yes, it is.
He has
been
very good.

Wink

w

23 in a party of 26 Antons

Wink went
and sat
in bed,
then
he fell
asleep.

Xray

x

24 in a party of 26 Antons

X-ray
cannot
run fast,
he has
big boots
on.

Yum-yum y

25 in a party of 26 Antons

Yum-yum
sat and
licked
his lips.
"Look my
food has
been
gobbled up."

Zip-zap

z

26 in a party of 26 Antons

Zip-zap
went fast
and had
fun, then
sat down
to catch
his breath.

the
way
out
nice
shop
play
food
good
been
chips
chair
going

likes
party
boots
catch
leader
winner
cuddly
number
asleep
breath
goggles
gobbled

Printed in Great Britain
by Amazon

38282878R10046